# JESSE OWENS
## FASTEST MAN ALIVE

**Carole Boston Weatherford**

ILLUSTRATED BY **Eric Velasquez**

BLOOMSBURY
CHILDREN'S BOOKS
NEW YORK  LONDON  OXFORD  NEW DELHI  SYDNEY

**ON YOUR MARK.**

READY. SET.

# GO!

Go from cotton fields to city sidewalks,
from sickly child to keen competitor,
from second-class citizen to first-place finish.
Go, Jesse, go.  Trounce Jim Crow.
Run as fast as your feet can fly,
as far as your dreams will reach.
Go across the ocean, bearing America's hopes.
Go to the Olympics; know that you will win.

## WILLKOMMEN

Welcome to Berlin, city of the future, Germany's jewel.
See cars zipping on autobahns, zeppelins
amidst clouds, and a television—
the first you've seen—
flickering fuzzy, gray pictures.
Make yourself at home in the Olympic Village.

Taste bratwurst; enjoy the bands and fireworks.
But know that Nazi flags
on storefronts do not fly for you.
Hitler does not want your kind here,
does not believe you belong.
Prove him wrong.

# BEYOND BERLIN

Do not look beyond Berlin.
You are not meant to see
the concentration camps
that hold the free-thinking souls
who dared to challenge Hitler's rise.
You are not meant to hear guns firing far away.
Still, you sense the evil.

For Hitler, these Olympics are *not* mere games
but a chance to show Germany's power to the world.
Hitler's hatred is a time bomb.
You hear it *tick-tick-ticking* as his armies march by.
This is not war—not yet.
For now, you will face *him* on the field.

## COUNTDOWN TO COMPETITION

You have just days to work off
your wobbly sea legs and
regain your footing on dry land,
just days to find new track shoes
to replace the ones you lost
in New York, just days to learn
a few German phrases to charm
the autograph hounds—
young fans who tap your
dormitory window.
They don't care what Hitler thinks,
and neither do you.

## OPENING CEREMONY

As you enter the stadium
before a crowd of thousands,
remember your mother's words:
*Put your best foot forward.*

How you wish she were here.
Dozens of flags file past
Hitler's viewing box.
Some delegations return his Nazi salute
and dip their banners,
but not the Americans;
Stars and Stripes remains upright.
As Germans stamp their feet
in anger, your heart races.
The parade marches on.

Then, the torch that crossed
seven nations lights the flame
to let the games begin.
Your face glows.
Only your goal is grander
than this moment.

# MEDAL #1: THE 100-METER DASH

Neither rain nor a muddy track
can douse your spirits today.
With five other sprinters—American, German, Swedish, Dutch—
you throw down your trowel, coil into a crouch,
and await the starting pistol.
Your every muscle listens. *Bang!*

You spring forward, striding in perfect rhythm,
keeping pace with the other five, pumping faster, faster.
Halfway through, you glide past your teammate,
crossing the finish line in just over ten seconds—
record time.
You win the race and untold hearts.

# ON THE VICTORY STAND

During your victory lap, the crowd cheers
*Yesseh Oh-vens! Yesseh Oh-vens!*
at once crowning a brown-skinned hero
and toppling Hitler's hopes
for Germany to sweep the games.

Later, you climb the victory stand.
A laurel wreath circles your head,
and "The Star Spangled Banner"
rings in your ears.
As the American flag is raised,
you fight back tears.

Hitler stays away that day,
preferring to congratulate no one
than to shake Black hands.
That is his loss.
In the leader's glaring absence
you do not miss for one moment
bowing to his stiff salute.
You hold your head high, opening
your arms to the adoring crowd.

After you clinch the gold, a hundred cameras flash;
your name is on newsmen's lips.
Fast fingers tap typewriters,
pecking praise from Paris to Pittsburgh.
The writers rave, calling you
"the Black arrow," "Black bullet,"
        "Black panther," "whirlwind."

Presses around the world
rush extra editions.
Headlines hailing your new record
leave readers breathless.
But you cannot let fame swell
your head or fog your sight.
You have races yet to run
and history still to write.

# A LEAP OF FRIENDSHIP

Tall, blond, blue-eyed Luz Long
limbers up while you look on.
The German leaps and alights,
landing in the finals
for the jump that bears his name.

You jog to shake the jitters,
warm the muscles, loosen joints.
But when you take off, the judges
rule you fouled twice.
Once more will mean elimination.

Long lends advice:
play it safe.
Make a mark before the board,
and jump from there.
Heeding his wisdom,
you sail to the pit—
nearly twenty-six feet—record distance.
One step closer to a medal.

Finally, Long versus Owens—
German and American
head-to-head in the long jump finals.
Long flows through his jump, flying as if on a trapeze.
You run through yours like an airplane at takeoff.
Inch by inch, you and Long push each other farther
than man has ever jumped.

Between jumps, you shake hands.
The lead shifts back and forth
as you and Long leap past each other.
Records stand but a round, then fall beneath winged feet.
In the end, you soar to a second gold medal, but Long is no sore loser.
He slaps your back, sealing the bond between you.
You two talk into the night; new friendship richer than gold.

From the sidelines, you study the starter
and notice his knees twitch before he pulls the trigger.
That will be your edge.
In the starting position, you eye those telltale knees.
The pistol fires; you bolt from the starting line,
feet barely brushing the track.

You round the curve, a racehorse trailed by thoroughbreds.
Five yards ahead of your teammate,
you burst through the tape
and into the record books.
Rain drenches the victory stand.
Fans shower you with cheers.

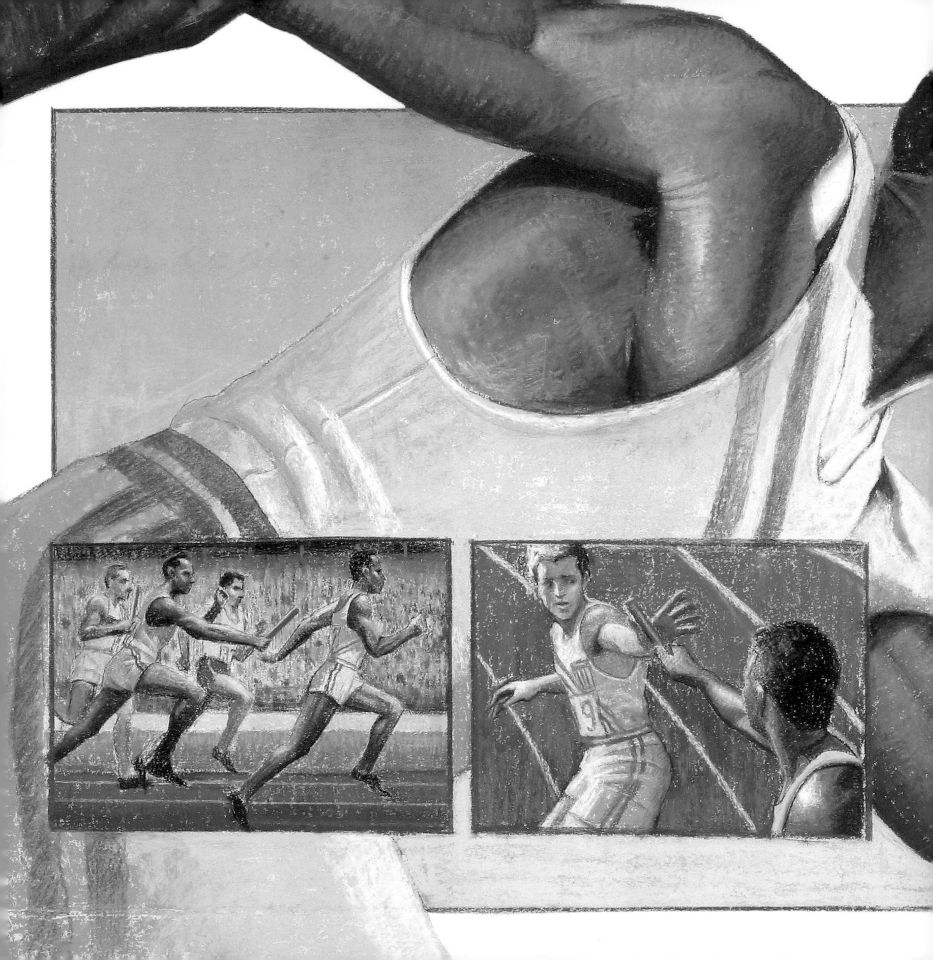

With three gold medals,
you could rest on your records,
but the Germans have saved
their fastest for last.
Your coaches need
a secret weapon—
you.

You run the first leg of the relay,
passing the baton and the lead
to the next runner.
By the finish line, the race
and your fourth medal are won.
Who'd have thought
that a sharecropper's son,
the grandson of slaves,
would crush Hitler's pride?
Who knew that you would trample
German might like a clod of dirt
in a field of glory?
Who'd have thought your star
would burn so bright?

# A HERO'S WELCOME

In London, you board the *Queen Mary,* a floating palace.
Your family meets the ocean liner in New York Harbor,
and Pop Riley, your old coach, greets you at the dock.
Their hugs wrap you with pride.
Tap dancer Bojangles whisks you uptown.
Harlem toasts you.

Parading up Broadway with your team,
you wave from the lead car like a prince.
Ticker tape streams from skyscrapers,
and for a few miles, the world is at your feet.
The records that you set stand for twenty-five years,
proving that you truly were the fastest man on earth.

## JESSE—BEYOND THE TRACK

Jesse Owens, the first American track-and-field athlete to win four gold medals in a single Olympics, is one of the most famous Olympic champions of all time. The son of a sharecropper and the grandson of a slave, James Cleveland Owens was born in 1913 in Oakville, Alabama. Known to his family as "J.C.," he grew up poor and sickly. The Owens family moved to Cleveland, Ohio, when J.C. was eight years old. At his new school, his teacher mistook his nickname for "Jesse," and the name stuck.

In Cleveland, Jesse's family was still poor, so young Jesse worked odd jobs in his spare time. During gym class, Coach Charlie Riley timed Jesse on the sixty-yard dash. Impressed by his speed, the coach invited Jesse to join the track team. Because Jesse had to work after school, Riley coached Jesse in the mornings. In 1928, Jesse's high jump and long jump, then known as the running broad jump, set junior high school world records. In high school, he won three straight state championships for track. As a senior, he set a world record in the 100-yard dash and was recruited by many colleges and universities.

Jesse chose to attend Ohio State University. As an African American student, he was barred from the dormitories and had to live off campus. On the road with the track team, he had to stay in Black hotels and eat at Black restaurants. But segregation did not slow him down. In 1935, despite injuries, Jesse set world records in the long jump, 220-yard dash, and 220-yard low hurdles. He also tied the record in the 100-yard dash. That same year, he married his childhood sweetheart, Ruth Solomon. They eventually had three daughters.

By 1936, Jesse had qualified for the United States track-and-field team and was a favorite for the Olympics in Berlin. At the time, Germany was ruled by Adolf Hitler, a powerful Nazi dictator whose hatred of Jews, Catholics, Jehovah's Witnesses, Roma, Communists, LGBTQ people, people with disabilities, and other non-Aryans soon sparked World War II. Hitler was sure that German athletes, whom he deemed superior, would dominate the Olympics. Jesse Owens dashed Hitler's hopes by winning the 100-meter dash, the 200-meter dash, the 400-meter relay, and the long jump. To Hitler's horror, the German spectators cheered Jesse on. In Berlin, he set two Olympic records and a world record for the long jump that stood for twenty-five years. He had shown that hard work, talent, and determination—regardless of the color of your skin—could triumph.

Back in the United States, Jesse was honored with a New York ticker-tape parade. Because he was African American, however, he did not get an endorsement deal as a paid company spokesperson. To support his family, he dropped out of college and ran races for money. He raced people, cars, motorcycles, and racehorses. Later, Jesse was Cleveland's playground director, a sought-after speaker, and the owner of a public relations firm.

In 1976, President Gerald Ford awarded Jesse Owens the Medal of Freedom, the nation's highest civilian honor. Jesse died in 1980. The Jesse Owens Foundation, which he formed to help underprivileged youth, still operates today.

## FURTHER READING

McKissack, Patricia, Fredrick McKissack, Michael David Biegel (ill.). *Jesse Owens: Olympic Star.* Berkeley Heights, NJ: Enslow Publishers, 1992.

Mezger, Gabi. *The Jesse Owens Story.* Des Moines, IA: Perfection Learning, 1997.

Nuwer, Hank. *The Legend of Jesse Owens.* New York, NY: Franklin Watts, 1998.

Raatma, Lucia. *Jesse Owens: Track-and-Field Olympian.* Chanhassen, MN: Child's World, 2003.

Streissguth, Thomas. *Jesse Owens.* Minneapolis, MN: Lerner Publications, 1999.

*For my family who have run this race with me.*
—C. B. W.

*For my bro Ernest A. Hernandez (1960–2004).*
*You will be missed.*
—E. V.

BLOOMSBURY CHILDREN'S BOOKS
Bloomsbury Publishing Inc., part of Bloomsbury Publishing Plc
1385 Broadway, New York, NY 10018

BLOOMSBURY, BLOOMSBURY CHILDREN'S BOOKS, and the Diana logo are trademarks of Bloomsbury Publishing Plc

First published in the United States of America in January 2007
by Walker Books for Young Readers, an imprint of Bloomsbury Publishing, Inc.
Paperback edition published in January 2022

Bloomsbury books may be purchased for business or promotional use. For information on bulk purchases
please contact Macmillan Corporate and Premium Sales Department at specialmarkets@macmillan.com

ISBN 978-1-5476-0898-0 (paperback)

The Library of Congress has cataloged the hardcover edition as follows:
Weatherford, Carole Boston. Jesse Owens : fastest man alive / Carole Boston Weatherford; illustrations by Eric Velasquez.
p.    cm.
ISBN-10: 0-8027-9550-1 • ISBN-13: 978-0-8027-9550-2 (hardcover)
ISBN-10: 0-8027-9551-X • ISBN-13: 978-0-8027-9551-9 (reinforced)
1. Owens, Jesse, 1913–80. 2. Track and field athletes—United States—Biography.  I. Velasquez, Eric. II. Title.
GV697.O9W43 2006      796.42092—dc22      2006010187

The illustrations for this book were created using Nupastels and soft pastels on prepared illustration board.
Book design by Amy Manzo Toth
Printed in China by C&C Offset Printing Co., Ltd., Shenzhen, Guangdong
2 4 6 8 10 9 7 5 3 1

To find out more about our authors and books visit www.bloomsbury.com and sign up for our newsletters.